SELF-WORTH
Discover Your
God-Given Worth

JUNE HUNT

ROSE PUBLISHING/ASPIRE PRESS

Torrance, California

ROSE PUBLISHING/ASPIRE PRESS

Self-Worth: Discover Your God-Given Worth
Copyright © 2013 Hope For The Heart
All rights reserved.
Aspire Press, a division of Rose Publishing, Inc.
4733 Torrance Blvd., #259
Torrance, California 90503 USA
www.aspirepress.com

Register your book at www.aspirepress.com/register
Get inspiration via email, sign up at www.aspirepress.com

The information and solutions offered in this resource are a result of
years of Bible study, research, and practical life application. They are
intended as guidelines for healthy living and are not a replacement
for professional counseling or medical advice. JUNE HUNT and
HOPE FOR THE HEART make no warranties, representations, or
guarantees regarding any particular result or outcome. Any and
all express or implied warranties are disclaimed. Please consult
qualified medical, pastoral, and psychological professionals regarding
individual conditions and needs. JUNE HUNT and HOPE FOR THE
HEART do not advocate that you treat yourself or someone you know
and disclaim any and all liability arising directly or indirectly from
the information in this resource.

For more information on Hope For The Heart, visit
www.hopefortheheart.org or call 1-800-488-HOPE (4673).

Printed by Regent Publishing Services Ltd.
Printed in China
January 2015, 5th printing

CONTENTS

ear friend,

Do you know what it's like to struggle with feelings of *low self-worth*? If so, I understand. In your heart of hearts, you believe you have little value—especially when compared to others. Regardless of how good you may look, you feel insignificant. For years, that was exactly how I felt.

As I look back on my childhood, I can see how my father shaped my reality—my view that I had little value. I *never* remember sitting on my father's lap, *never* heard, "*I love you,*" *never* heard, "*You did well.*" In fact, he never talked *with* me. He simply wasn't interested.

At dinnertime, Dad enforced the old adage: "Children are to be seen—not heard." He announced that we couldn't speak unless we had something of interest to say to everyone at the table. Of course, he wasn't interested in anything we had to say, so we rarely spoke.

His continual verbal and emotional abuse toward my mother wounded my spirit. The "put-downs" and painful accusations pierced my heart because my mother was the dearest person in my life.

Then one day, after coming home from high school, I realized, *I'm not really showing interest in him. I'm just focusing on his faults and on my pain. So instead of being bitter, I'm going to focus attention on him.* (Although he had never asked about *my* day, I decided I would ask about *his* day.)

Dad always drove home at 5:45 p.m. and expected to have dinner at 6:00 sharp. So when I heard him walk into the side entrance of the house, I was ready—I had primed my pump for my positive greeting.

Inside the narrow hallway, I confidently approached him with a smile and said, *"Hi Dad, how was your day?"*

He exploded and yelled, *"Don't ever ask me that question! That's a stupid question! Never ask me that again!"*

Blown away, I felt humiliated and hurt. He had just used a stun gun on my heart. Even today, I can still feel the heat of his volcanic reaction on my cheeks.

Please understand—I am well aware that this encounter is so minor, especially in light of the major abuse that many experience. Yet encounters like this can be almost as *emotionally* paralyzing as physical and sexual abuse. I still recall his harshness—his yelling, his scowling—as though it were yesterday. How vividly I remember its demoralizing impact on my sense of significance! And never again did I ask him about his day.

It's painful to feel like a nonperson—to feel invisible, to feel insignificant.

But realize, God knows when you have a skewed view of yourself—and He cares. The Bible says, *"The Lord is close to the brokenhearted and saves those who are crushed in spirit"* (Psalm 34:18).

It's a great help just to know that the Lord holds you close when your heart has been hurt. But it's also vital that you know *what God says about you is true.*

According to the Word of God:

▶ God chose to create you, and as the old saying goes, *"God don't make no junk!"*

"God created man in his own image."
(Genesis 1:27)

▶ God has a plan for your life, and *He took His time to plan it.*

"'I know the plans I have for you,' declares the LORD, 'plans to prosper you and not to harm you, plans to give you hope and a future.'"
(Jeremiah 29:11)

▶ God loves you, and He will never stop loving you.

"I have loved you with an everlasting love; I have drawn you with loving-kindness."
(Jeremiah 31:3)

Knowing just these three truths has helped me immeasurably. Even if we periodically have difficulty *feeling* God's love—because our emotions can get stuck—*we can know He loves us.* Even if we sometimes struggle with *feeling* insignificant, *we can know we have worth.* You are so significant that Jesus chose to die for you. Think about it: *You don't die for something that has no worth!*

A major key to overcoming my struggle with self-worth has been *changing my focus* from the rejection of my earthly father to the love of my heavenly Father, *changing my focus* from my painful family life to the reality that I'm in the family of God, *changing my focus* from demoralizing personal failures to the fact that Jesus is my personal Redeemer.

If you can't see your *God-given value*, if you wonder about your *God-given worth*, you've come to the right place. Within these pages you'll learn what is true about you. As you read, I pray that His love will transform every false view you have until you are able to see yourself as God sees you: His precious child of infinite worth.

Yours in the Lord's hope,

June

June Hunt

SELF-WORTH
Discover Your
God-Given Worth

What happens when you long to receive a gift, but only your sister is given a gift? What happens when you long to be held on your mother's lap, but only your sister is allowed on her lap? What happens when you long for your mother's love, but only your sister is given her love?

Ask Dorie Van Stone.[1] Dorie would tell you that repeated rejection is the breeding ground for low self-worth. Her own mother never even wanted her. Her own mother always called her "ugly."

Dorie never received the love and affection her heart so deeply craved. However, what a comfort for Dorie (and for all the Dories in the world, both male and female) to come to know this truth:

> "The LORD does not look at
> the things man looks at.
> Man looks at the outward appearance,
> but the LORD looks at the heart."
> (1 Samuel 16:7)

DEFINITIONS

Why *should* Dorie feel any sense of worth? Even before she and her sister were discarded at an orphanage, life with their mother was filled with rejection. Her mother would leave Dorie in charge of her little sister for hours—a six-year-old responsible for the total care of a five-year-old! Each time, she longed desperately for her mother to return, saying to herself, "I hope she'll be glad to see me." But each time her mother returned, she brushed right past Dorie to gather Marie into her arms and give her a great big hug, sometimes bringing a gift, always showering attention—attention never shown to Dorie. No wonder Dorie was left reeling with low self-worth.[2] As the psalmist said ...

> **"Scorn has broken my heart
> and has left me helpless;
> I looked for sympathy, but there was none,
> for comforters, but I found none."
> (Psalm 69:20)**

As a child, Dorie didn't have any concept of "self-worth." How could she? As a continually rejected child, how could she feel any sense of significance, of value, of worth? Even more basic than that, how do you determine the worth of something or someone? How do you know your own worth? Do you look to yourself or others in order to grasp your value? If you look anywhere other than to God—the God who created you with a purpose and a plan—your view of your own value is in grave danger of being distorted. Before you were ever born, God established your real worth by knowing you, by choosing you, and ultimately by dying for you! The Bible says ...

> **"He chose us in him before the creation**
> **of the world to be holy**
> **and blameless in his sight."**
> **(Ephesians 1:4)**

▶ **Worth** signifies the value, merit, or significance of a person or thing.[3]

▶ **Self-worth** is the belief that your life has value and significance.[4]

▶ "**Worth**" is a translation of the Greek word *axios*, which means "of weight and worth."[5] In biblical times, gold and other precious metals were placed on a balancing scale where their worth was determined by their weight, leading to the expression, *"worth their weight in gold"* (Lamentations 4:2).

QUESTION: "How can someone's worth be determined?"

ANSWER: At an auction, the worth of an item is determined clearly and simply by one thing: the highest price paid. Each item goes to the highest bidder. You were bought from the auction block of sin over 2,000 years ago when the heavenly Father paid the highest price possible—the life of His Son, Jesus Christ. By that one act, your worth was forever established by God.

Jesus Christ paid the ultimate price for you—willingly dying on the cross—paying the penalty for your sins. He loves you that much! Your true worth is not based on anything *you* have done or will do, but on what *Jesus* has *already done*. Without a doubt, He established your worth. You were worth His life. You were worth dying for.

"This is how God showed his love among us:
He sent his one and only Son into the world
that we might live through him.
This is love: not that we loved God,
but that he loved us and sent his Son
as an atoning sacrifice for our sins."
(1 John 4:9–10)

In Dorie's younger years, not one person valued her; no one found pleasure in her, and she found favor with no one. Since no one esteemed her, she had no sense of self-esteem. She could easily see which of the other children were treated with value and, as a result, felt valuable themselves. Her sister was one of these highly favored ones.[6]

What makes you feel good about yourself? Do you consider your opinions worthy of consideration? Do you expect others to respect your boundaries, or do you hold yourself in such low esteem that you do not establish and maintain healthy boundaries—boundaries that line up with God's purpose for your life? The Bible says ...

> "Above all else, guard your heart,
> for it is the wellspring of life."
> (Proverbs 4:23)

▶ **To esteem** means "to set a high value on."[7]

▶ **"To esteem"** is a translation of the Hebrew *hasab*, which means "to consider, plan, reckon, or think over."[8]

▶ **To have self-esteem** is to respect or have high regard for yourself.[9]

> "He [Messiah] was despised,
> and we esteemed him not."
> (Isaiah 53:3)

QUESTION: "Why do some people prefer not to focus on self-esteem—but only on self-worth?"

ANSWER: The word *self-esteem* actually has two different meanings that are opposite to each other.

▶ The first is an *objective regard of your value* which the Bible refers to as *humility*. This self-worth is rooted in the recognition of your sins and your need for the Savior, recognition of your need to live dependently on Him, and of the fact that Christ established your worth by dying for you.

"This is the one I esteem: he who is humble and contrite in spirit, and trembles at my word." (Isaiah 66:2)

▶ The second kind of self-esteem is an *exaggerated regard of your value* which the Bible refers to as *pride*. This self-esteem is rooted in the idea that you are "good enough" within yourself to meet your own needs and therefore you do not need to live dependently on the Savior. Your worth is established by your "inherent goodness" and "personal accomplishments." But the Bible says, *"Do not be arrogant... Do not be proud... Do not be conceited."* (Romans 11:20; 12:16)

In the Bible, God presents these two types of "self-esteem" in sharp contrast to one another.

> **"God opposes the proud**
> **but gives grace to the humble."**
> **(1 Peter 5:5)**

How could Dorie *not* feel inferior when for years she was continuously treated as inferior? Emblazoned in her memory are scenes of her mother tucking her sister into bed saying, "Marie is a pretty girl—she's not like you." Then after tenderly kissing Marie, she would callously walk past Dorie.[10]

Repeated times of rejection are the building blocks of an inferiority complex. Someone with such low self-worth could easily think, *"Because of all my enemies, I am the utter contempt of my neighbors; I am a dread to my friends—those who see me on the street flee from me. I am forgotten by them as though I were dead; I have become like broken pottery"* (Psalm 31:11–12).

▶ An **inferiority complex**[11] is a painful, debilitating feeling of being less valuable than others.

- *Inferior* means less valued than others.

- A *complex* is a group of beliefs based on the past that has a powerful influence on present behavior.

▶ An **inferiority complex** is an acute sense of low self-worth, which has two very different results:

- *Fearfully timid* attitudes and actions as a result of giving in to others or feeling rejected by others: "I'm nothing. I know I don't matter."

- *Overly aggressive* attitudes and actions to compensate for feeling rejected: "Since people hate me, I'll give them something to hate!"

In the orphanage, Dorie became the bitter bully who punched and pinched the other children just to make them cry. Openly hostile, Dorie used fear tactics to get her way—and get her way she did![12] Although she was young, her life mirrored this Psalm:

> "When my heart was grieved and my spirit embittered, I was senseless and ignorant; I was a brute beast before you."
> (Psalm 73:21–22)

A Self-Worth Struggler

2 Samuel chapter 9

Mephibosheth felt like the weakest link in the royal chain. Crippled in both feet at a young age, he never felt able to live up to the accomplishments of his family. His grandfather, King Saul, was a fierce warrior. His father, Jonathan, was an accomplished soldier.

But Mephibosheth was unable to stand on his own two feet, let alone to do battle. Following the deaths of both Saul and Jonathan, when David claimed the throne, Mephibosheth sank into financial and emotional quicksand. He lived in the land of Lo-Debar, which means "the House of No Bread." While his family had ruled a nation and enjoyed substantial wealth, he ended up with nothing. From the palace to poverty, since he could not even afford his own lodging, he lived in another man's home.

King David summons Mephibosheth to appear before his throne. Mephibosheth knows his life has no value. After a change in dynasty, the custom of the day was to execute the previous royal line. He knows King David can kill him on the spot to eliminate any competition for the throne.

Mephibosheth feels helpless and hopeless. He shuffles on his lame feet, crawling into the new king's house to answer David's summons. He throws himself on the ground before David declaring himself to be nothing more than a *"dead dog."* David's response shocked the young cripple who had known little kindness in his life. *"'Don't be afraid,' David said to him, 'for I will surely show you kindness for the sake of your father Jonathan. I will restore to you all the land that belonged to your grandfather Saul, and you will always eat at my table'"* (2 Samuel 9:7).

Imagine his astonishment! David—the feared warrior-king—had demonstrated compassion to a cripple. But why—why toward this weak invalid who was, in his own words *"a dead dog,"* one who could offer no service to the king, one who was a reminder of his grandfather's murderous vengeance directed toward David? Because long before, David had entered into a covenant relationship with Jonathan, a covenant commitment, a covenant vow of loyalty that extends even to the family of Jonathan. And as David promised, *"Mephibosheth ate at David's table like one of the king's sons"* (2 Samuel 9:11). Picture the household of David gathering for an evening meal. The aristocratic and selfish yet powerful Amnon, the proud and handsome Absalom with his beautiful sister Tamar, the scholarly, withdrawn and poetic person of Solomon. Then shuffling along behind them and taking his place among the king's sons and daughters at the finest table in the land is this *"dead dog"* Mephibosheth. He may have once felt worthless and utterly without value, but because of the king's grace, he discovered his infinite worth.

If you suffer from feelings of inferiority—feeling like an emotional cripple—know that the King of Kings in His grace has reached out to you with care and compassion to *adopt you into His family* and take you as His own. As a member of the family of Christ, you have a place reserved at the King's table forever. Make no mistake, you *are* no mistake. Not only are you wanted, but you also have immeasurable worth. The Bible even says ...

"In love he predestined us to be adopted as his sons through Jesus Christ, in accordance with his pleasure and will." (Ephesians 1:4–5)

Clearly, Dorie struggled with having no sense of self-worth. Some people would say she should not have self-worth—that's prideful. Others say she should have more self-worth—that's healthy. Which is right—especially from a Christian standpoint?

Is there a place in the life of a Christian for self-respect, self-worth, and self-love, or does the Bible exhort us to disrespect, devalue, and even hate ourselves? The Bible appears to support both self-love and self-hate, a seeming contradiction that has resulted in a very real controversy. Since the Bible cannot contradict itself, we need godly discernment to know how to think about ourselves accurately. We learn from Proverbs ...

"The wise in heart are called discerning, and pleasant words promote instruction." (Proverbs 16:21)

The Three Views

1 I should not love myself.

"It's wrong for me to love my own life. Instead, I should hate myself."

Biblical support:

"The man who loves his life will lose it, while the man who hates his life in this world will keep it for eternal life." (John 12:25)

2 **I should love myself.**

"God tells me in His Word that it is appropriate to love myself."

Biblical support:

"Love your neighbor as yourself."
(Leviticus 19:18)

This commandment is found twice in Leviticus, then repeated in six other books of the Bible.

- Leviticus 19:18, 34
- Matthew 19:19; 22:39
- Mark 12:31, 33
- Luke 10:27
- Romans 13:9
- Galatians 5:14
- James 2:8

3 **I don't know whether I should love myself, but I do know I should love others.**

"Scripture is confusing about self-love, but I know I should have sacrificial love for others."

Biblical support:

"This is how we know what love is: Jesus Christ laid down his life for us. And we ought to lay down our lives for our brothers." (1 John 3:16)

Two Major Questions

QUESTION #1: "In Luke 14:26, does the Bible really mean for me to hate my family and myself?"

ANSWER: To interpret any literary work correctly, a major principle of interpretation must be applied: *context*! Therefore, look at how "hatred" is used in context of the whole counsel of God's Word.

▶ Moses states, *"Do not hate your brother in your heart."* (Leviticus 19:17)

▶ The Ten Commandments state, *"Honor your father and your mother"*—not *hate* your father and mother! (Exodus 20:12)

▶ The apostle John states, *"Anyone who claims to be in the light but hates his brother is still in the darkness."* (1 John 2:9)

▶ Jesus states, astonishing those who hear Him, *"You have heard that it was said, 'Love your neighbor and hate your enemy.' But I tell you: Love your enemies and pray for those who persecute you."* (Matthew 5:43–44)

CONCLUSION: Based on the *whole counsel of God*, we are *not* to carry hatred in our hearts. When referring to hating our father, mother, sister, brother—and even our own lives—Jesus was not promoting a lifestyle of personal hatred. Such a message is completely inconsistent with the heart of the Bible and the heart of the Lord.

Jesus instead appealed to His followers to hate anything—including anything in their own lives—that stood in the way of giving their relationship with Him absolute priority. If we are to be true disciples, Jesus must be preeminent—Jesus must occupy the place of highest priority. We should not let anyone take the place that He alone should have.

The apostle Paul builds a case for placing Christ in this priority:

"By him all things were created: things in heaven and on earth, visible and invisible, whether thrones or powers or rulers or authorities; all things were created by him and for him. He is before all things, and in him all things hold together. And he is the head of the body, the church; he is the beginning and the firstborn from among the dead, so that in everything he might have the supremacy."
(Colossians 1:16–18)

QUESTION #2: "Since the Bible says, 'Love your neighbor as yourself,' am I actually supposed to love myself, or is that arrogance and pride?"

ANSWER: When we hear the word *love*, we usually assume it means *affectionate love* or *passionate love*, but *agape love* is the type of love referred to in this passage. The Greek word *agape* in the text means a "commitment to do what is best on behalf of others." If you truly *"love your neighbor as yourself,"* you must comprehend the context of this love as well as understand its roots.

▶ Jesus presents the two most important commandments: *"'Love the Lord your God with all your heart and with all your soul and with all your mind and with all your strength.' The second is this: 'Love your neighbor as yourself.' There is no commandment greater than these."* (Mark 12:30–31)

▶ The apostle Paul states that love is the fulfillment of the law: *"Love does no harm to its neighbor. Therefore love is the fulfillment of the law."* (Romans 13:10)

▶ We are to love with *agape* love, which is based not on feeling, but on commitment. *"If you love those who love you, what credit is that to you? Even 'sinners' love those who love them. ... But love your enemies, do good to them, and lend to them without expecting to get anything back. Then your reward will be great, and you will be sons of the Most High, because he is kind to the ungrateful and wicked."* (Luke 6:32, 35)

▶ We are to love what God loves, that is, we are to value the truth that God loves us. *"We love because he first loved us."* (1 John 4:19)

CONCLUSION: The Bible says, *"God is love"* (1 John 4:8). The essence of God is *agape*—a love that always seeks the highest and best on behalf of others. If we are truly godly—and we are told to be godly—then we will value what He values and love what He loves. We are to love the fact that He has a purpose for us. We are to love the fact that He values us. We are to love the fact that He has given us worth.

▶ You have godly *agape* for yourself when you do what God says is best for you, cooperating with His perfect plan for your life.

▶ And you have *agape* for those around you by doing what is consistent with God's very best for them.

"'Love the Lord your God with all your heart and with all your soul and with all your mind.' This is the first and greatest commandment. And the second is like it: 'Love your neighbor as yourself.'" (Matthew 22:37–39)

CHARACTERISTICS OF LOW SELF-WORTH

In the throes of threatening circumstances, people react in one of three ways: fight, flight, or freeze—get even, get going, or get hurt. Those who fight can quickly become aggressive victimizers. Because she was beaten and abused, Dorie chose to become defiant, to clench her fists and dominate her peers by intimidation.

She would bully them into compliance, threatening to "get them in the yard" if they didn't drink her buttermilk for her or let her go to the front of the bathing line. She forced her will on them and terrorized them by pinching or hitting them without provocation. According to her own words, "I was mean, mean, mean!"

Because Dorie *knew* that no one would ever love her, she took the offensive and gave them no reason to love her. She cried alone at night and made others cry during the day. No one would get the best of her, no one! She had no one, so she would need no one. That was her philosophy, at least until the day she met Jesus and opened her heart to His life-changing love. He gave her a new heart.[13] The Lord makes this offer to everyone:

"I will give you a new heart and put a new spirit in you; I will remove from you your heart of stone and give you a heart of flesh."
(Ezekiel 36:26)

When Dorie went to grade school, she said, "Those of us from the orphanage could be easily identified by our shabby clothes and distinctive haircuts." The harsh matron, Miss Gabriel, would place a bowl on their heads and snip off their hair with other children and parents staring. Dorie thought, "We're all oddballs and besides, I'm ugly." It's as though she kept looking through distorted mirrors.[14]

Think about going to a fair and walking through "The Fun House" with its warped mirrors. When you turn the corner, you suddenly see a distorted image of yourself that immediately makes you laugh. Your head looks like a huge oval egg with narrow slanted eyes. Meanwhile, your neck has disappeared. Your arms have become wavy tentacles and your hips the size of a blimp.

Unfortunately, people like Dorie walk around with mental images of themselves that are as warped as these distorted mirrors. Over time, their inner mirror has become warped by criticism, disapproval, and pain. Thank God He does not look at us from a warped perspective, but through the eyes of purest love. The closer we are to Him, the more we will be able to see ourselves through God's eyes. The Bible says, *"Now we see but a poor reflection as in a mirror; then we shall see face to face. Now I know in part; then I shall know fully, even as I am fully known"* (1 Corinthians 13:12).

Checklist for Low Self-Worth

To determine whether you are suffering with low self-worth, place a check mark (√) by the statements below that are true about you.

Inner Insecurities

☐ I am self-critical and have feelings of self-loathing.

☐ I am fearful of failure and avoid risk-taking.

☐ I am overly impacted by the opinions of others and strive to meet their standards.

☐ I am undeserving of and yet desperate for the approval of others.

☐ I am unhappy with my personal appearance and personal achievements.

☐ I am negligent of my appearance.

☐ I am unable to set boundaries.

☐ I am ashamed of my background, and I often struggle with depression.

☐ I am controlled by a victim mentality.

☐ I am inferior and incompetent when compared to others.

If you struggle with insecurity, you need to take to heart these words of encouragement from the Word of God:

"Be strong and courageous. Do not be afraid ... for the LORD your God goes with you; he will never leave you nor forsake you." (Deuteronomy 31:6)

Relational Roadblocks

☐ I am overly critical and distrustful of others.

☐ I am demanding and unforgiving of others.

☐ I am defensive when confronted.

☐ I am argumentative and resistant to authority.

☐ I am undeserving of and unable to accept compliments.

☐ I am afraid to get close to people and establish intimacy.

☐ I am a peace-at-all-costs people pleaser.

☐ I am reluctant to express my true feelings.

☐ I am hesitant to accept responsibility for my wrongs.

☐ I am often afraid to defend myself.

If you struggle with establishing healthy relationships, you need to know that ...

**"Fear of man will prove to be a snare,
but whoever trusts in the Lord is kept safe."
(Proverbs 29:25)**

Although Dorie was powerless to prevent unjustified beatings at the oppressive orphanage, she learned how to get power by overpowering the other children. This gave her the feeling of significance—a sense of self-worth.

"If I can be tough," she reasoned, "I can survive. I bullied the other children. I was never subtle. I pushed and shoved. I hit. If another child wouldn't let me see his toy, I would grab it. The others didn't hit me, but I hit them and felt good about it." [15]

All of this false bravado merely served as a substitute for true self-worth—a quick fix that was really not a fix.

If you are suffering with low self-worth, you may be seeking ways to deny, disguise, or diminish your emotional pain. People cope with their woundedness in different ways; however, many of these ways do not offer a cure, but rather are a counterfeit, an adhesive bandage that only covers up the wound without healing it.

The problem with "self-worth substitutes" is that they do not deal with the cause of the pain—the wrong beliefs that fester in the heart and mind. The true solution to low self-worth is to apply the healing balm of truth to the wound in the soul in order that your mind will be transformed and your life changed. Therefore, beware of worldly substitutes that ultimately do not satisfy.

"Do not love the world or anything in the world. If anyone loves the world, the love of the Father is not in him. For everything in the world—the cravings of sinful man, the lust of his eyes and the boasting of what he has and does—comes not from the Father but from the world. The world and its desires pass away, but the man who does the will of God lives forever."
(1 John 2:15–17)

Self-Worth Substitutes

If you are suffering with low self-worth and think you may be pursuing a substitute to make up for an emotional deficit, place a check mark (√) by the statements below that are true about you.

☐ I am impressed with status symbols and often live beyond my income.

☐ I am overly competitive and view losing as a reflection of my value and worth.

☐ I am seeking approval and am envious of important people.

☐ I am constantly striving for recognition.

☐ I am perfectionistic in an attempt to earn approval.

☐ I am addicted to substances, sex, food, and/or _____ .

☐ I am angry and intimidating at times in a zeal to accomplish my goals.

☐ I am financially extravagant in an attempt to impress others.

☐ I am obsessed with having certain possessions.

☐ I am insistent on getting my way.

If you struggle with any of these substitutes, ask yourself this question:

> **"What good is it for a man to gain the whole world, yet forfeit his soul?"**
> **(Mark 8:36)**

At the orphanage, Miss Gabriel believed that sickness was always a result of sin. Therefore, whenever Dorie became ill, the stern matron would snap, "It's the Lord! He's punishing you. If you weren't so naughty, you wouldn't be sick." A harsh, punishing God was the only kind of heavenly Father Dorie ever heard about. She heard nothing about His love.[16]

Those who have a warped view of themselves often have a warped view of God. When people feel unworthy of love, respect, and approval from others, often they feel even more unworthy of God's love, respect, and approval. Their faulty beliefs lead them to draw faulty conclusions about God. These wrong beliefs about God serve only to sabotage their relationship with God and kill any hope of ever being valued or used by God.

> **"There is a way that seems right to a man, but in the end it leads to death." (Proverbs 14:12)**

Spiritual Sabotages

If you suffer with low self-worth and feel concerned about your relationship with God, place a check mark (√) by the statements below that are true of you.

☐ I have difficulty feeling acceptable to God.

☐ I have difficulty admitting my guilt to God.

☐ I have difficulty forgiving God.

☐ I have difficulty trusting God.

☐ I have difficulty accepting the forgiveness of God.

☐ I have difficulty living in the grace of God.

☐ I have difficulty feeling loved by God.

☐ I have difficulty feeling wanted by God.

☐ I have difficulty thinking God has designed a special plan for me.

☐ I have difficulty believing the promises of God are for me.

If you are struggling spiritually, wondering about the reality and role of God in your life, you need to know that ...

"The LORD is close to the brokenhearted and saves those who are crushed in spirit."
(Psalm 34:18)

QUESTION: "How could a loving God allow abuse?"

ANSWER: God did not create people to be puppets but to be free agents, able to make their own choices. In granting people that freedom, He knew people would choose to sin against Him and against one another. Make no mistake: God is not the abuser. He hates the evil of abuse and will one day repay those who do evil.

"I will punish the world for its evil, the wicked for their sins. I will put an end to the arrogance of the haughty and will humble the pride of the ruthless."
(Isaiah 13:11)

CAUSES OF LOW SELF-WORTH

For many reasons people fail to perceive themselves as having value or worth to God, to themselves, or to others. Generally, negative self-perceptions develop in people as a result of their being treated in ways that cause them to feel devalued by significant people in their lives. Unless these perceptions are changed, self-devaluation will worsen over time.

Negative perceptions that begin in childhood are difficult to replace with positive perceptions in adulthood. The best time to examine and evaluate self-worth is before self-perceptions become strong and solidified.

As in the case of Dorie, the more she was rejected, the more she rejected herself and those around her. Her greatest need was to have someone accept her and value her as a person, someone to heal her emotional wounds and to cause her to see her significance. That Someone turned out to be the true Healer of the brokenhearted.

> "He heals the brokenhearted
> and binds up their wounds."
> (Psalm 147:3)

When Dorie and her sister were left at the orphanage, her mother promised to visit them. And she did—twice over a span of seven years. At the first visit, Dorie, exuding immense excitement, immediately ran to her calling out, "Mother! Mother!" In her exhilaration, Dorie had forgotten she was to call her mother "Laura," never "Mother."[17]

Repeating her past pattern, this "Laura" pushed Dorie aside only to greet her sister with both a hug and a gift. Such harsh, heartless rejection of Dorie by her mother continued throughout her mother's lifetime.

The roots of rejection are not always easily uncovered, especially when their tentacles reach deep into childhood. Those who are rejected from conception can have a lifelong experience of never feeling loved and accepted, of never knowing the comfort of a mother's warm, reassuring embrace or the security of a father's strong, protecting arms.

When rejection is all that has been known, identifying its origins can feel overwhelming and frightening. But if rejection is to be removed from your life, it must be fearlessly faced and dug up by the roots with the help of the Lord and replaced with His loving acceptance.

> "This is what the LORD says—
> he who made you,
> who formed you in the womb,
> and who will help you:
> Do not be afraid."
> (Isaiah 44:2)

The actions and attitudes of parents toward their children send clear messages to children about their value and worth—not just their value to their parents, but their value and worth as human beings. These messages "stick like glue" and carry lifelong implications. The Bible says ...

> "Do not embitter your children,
> or they will become discouraged."
> (Colossians 3:21)

MESSAGES CHILDREN RECEIVE FROM ADDICTED PARENTS

▶ Chemically dependent parents: "Their alcohol/ drugs are more important than I am."

▶ Workaholic parents: "Their work is more important than I am."

▶ Compulsive spending parents: "Their money and things are more important than I am."

▶ Perfectionistic parents: "Their demand for perfection is more important than I am."

Messages Children Receive from Abusive Parents

▶ Emotionally abusive parents: "I am a nobody."

▶ Verbally abusive parents: "I am deserving of put-downs."

▶ Physically abusive parents: "I am meant to be a punching bag."

▶ Sexually abusive parents: "I am nothing more than a sex object."

> **"He stands at the right hand
> of the needy one."**
> **(Psalm 109:31)**

MYTH: "I will never overcome my painful past—it's impossible for me to become whole."

TRUTH: No matter what your past was like or the pain inflicted on you by others, healing and wholeness are possible through Christ.

> **"With God all things are possible."**
> **(Matthew 19:26)**

Dorie writes about monthly visits to the orphanage by couples looking to adopt a child. "My dread of those 'special days' escalated month by month. No doubt I reflected the rejection I felt. My shoulders drooped with the agony of that lineup. I could not look up with smiling anticipation as the cute children did. I detested being inspected by people I knew would never accept me, so I would hide. I would be dragged into the room with a dirty, tear-stained face."[18]

Thankfully, Dorie's story does not end with her not being chosen by these people, for she was chosen by Another, by God Himself, as stated in James 2:5: *"Has not God chosen those who are poor in the eyes of the world to be rich in faith and to inherit the kingdom he promised those who love him?"*

Those who repeatedly experience significant rejection by others receive the message that they deserve rejection. Then they internalize that message and begin to reject themselves. This is especially true when rejection comes from those who are in positions of authority and on whom the child depends.

Such children grow up replaying in their minds the recorded messages/tapes of rejection they have received until the voices on the tapes become their own voices. It is virtually impossible for children to replace the big booming voices of adults/parents with their own small, inner voices.

Only the loving, accepting voice of God is powerful enough to override and eventually silence voices with messages of rejection—and thus salvage the self-worth of these rejected children. Only God can bring them to the point of saying ...

> "Though my father and mother forsake me, the LORD will receive me." (Psalm 27:10)

MESSAGES CHILDREN RECEIVE FROM PARENTS AND AUTHORITY FIGURES

▶ Overly critical: "I am incompetent."

▶ Overly protective: "I am inadequate."

▶ Overly controlling: "I am unacceptable."

▶ Overly permissive: "I am not valuable."

MESSAGES CHILDREN RECEIVE FROM SIBLINGS AND PEERS

▶ Overly critical: "I am inferior."

▶ Discouraging: "I am hopeless."

▶ Pushy: "I am weak."

▶ Overly competitive: "I am inept."

MESSAGES CHILDREN RECEIVE FROM SOCIETY

▶ Overly competitive attitudes: "I am insecure."

▶ Materialistic: "I am unimportant."

▶ Academic or physical limitations: "I am insignificant."

▶ Racial or sexual discrimination: "I am rejected."

Have you let negative circumstances shape your thinking and self-perceptions? If so, allow God to search your heart in order to reveal any perceptions/messages that are inconsistent with His Word. The more you allow God's probing light to illumine the faulty thoughts and perceptions in your heart, the more you will be able to see your God-given worth and walk victoriously according to His Word. Let this be your commitment.

"We demolish arguments and every pretension that sets itself up against the knowledge of God, and we take captive every thought to make it obedient to Christ."
(2 Corinthians 10:5)

MYTH: "Because of the way I've been treated, I will never feel competent."

TRUTH: Since people fail people, God never intended your competence to come from other people. As you continue to yield your life to the Lord, your competence will come from Him.

"Not that we are competent in ourselves to claim anything for ourselves, but our competence comes from God."
(2 Corinthians 3:5)

Dorie's life was a perfect setup for comparing herself to others. Her mother constantly compared her to her sister, resulting in her little sister receiving lavish affection and gifts from their mother and Dorie being pointedly ignored. Her mother verbally let her know that she did not measure up. Everywhere Dorie turned, Marie was the favored one. Thus, Marie was everything Dorie wanted to be. Both had brown eyes, but Marie's were beautiful. Both had dark hair, but Marie's lay in place. Marie's skin was fairer, her face thinner. Dorie said, "I was looking for a way to be like her, but there was no way."[19]

At the orphanage, in school, and in the various foster homes where they lived, other children were chosen or received decent treatment while Dorie was rejected and subjected to abuse. Dorie described the couples who came to the orphanage considering which child they would choose—which child they would cherish—as "well-dressed and carefully manicured. We could hear their muffled conversations, 'She's cute, isn't she?' or, 'There's one we might want to talk about.' My heart beat faster. 'Try me,' I screamed within, hoping that someone would look at me and want me. But my day never came. I soon got the message—only cute children are chosen."

Dorie lost out every time she was compared to the other children. She was never chosen—never—

not once.[20] How could she *not* compare herself to others under those circumstances?

However, God had a plan for Dorie, and He would work out His purpose, His will for her life. The Bible makes this clear:

> **"In him we were also chosen, having been predestined according to the plan of him who works out everything in conformity with the purpose of his will."**
> **(Ephesians 1:11)**

Has comparing yourself to others become so automatic that you hardly notice you're doing it? People often compare themselves to others in appearance, abilities, affluence, and accomplishments. Read the statements below to see whether they have become part of your self-talk.

APPEARANCE

▶ Physical features: "I am not as attractive as …"

▶ Clothes: "I cannot dress as nicely as …"

▶ Mannerisms: "I am not as graceful or suave as …"

ABILITIES

▶ Physical abilities: "I am not as athletic as …"

▶ Mental abilities: "I am not as smart as …"

▶ Social abilities: "I am not as popular as …"

AFFLUENCE

▶ Financial/job status: "I am not as financially secure as …"

▶ Family status: "I don't have a home as nice as …"

▶ Social status: "I am not as influential as …"

ACCOMPLISHMENTS

▶ Education: "I don't have as many degrees as …"

▶ Talent: "I am not as gifted as …"

▶ Recognition: "I am not as accomplished as …"

MYTH: "I'll never be able to stop comparing myself to others."

TRUTH: Life is a series of choices, and while you may feel that you cannot change, God would not instruct you to do something without giving you the power to do it. God says if you compare yourself to others, you are not wise.

"When they measure themselves by themselves and compare themselves with themselves, they are not wise."
(2 Corinthians 10:12)

WHY IS Wrong Thinking So Wrong?

Dorie had every reason to develop wrong thinking and form faulty perceptions of herself. From her earliest memories, all she was told was that she didn't do anything right, that everything was her fault, that she wasn't good enough, that no one loved her or found value in her. Besides all that, she knew she was ugly. She thought, "I must be the ugliest child that ever walked. I felt so ugly on the inside that I believed I was ugly on the outside ... maybe it's my curly hair or my nose!"[21]

Do you go through life fearing what others think? Some people look in the mirror and see only an ugly duckling—a sad little bird with no self-worth. In her early years, Dorie considered herself the "ugly duckling"—ugly, unadoptable Dorie. Not only was she called ugly, but she also felt ugly because of the repeated pain of rejection.

In Hans Christian Andersen's fairy tale "The Ugly Duckling," the title character felt rejected and rebuffed by all the barnyard birds because they didn't like his looks or his awkward waddle. He didn't see the beautiful swan that was within, although the beauty was there all along.

In truth, many people suffer from self-rejection, thinking they possess no personal value. Yet like this young little duckling, they look only to their outer image to determine their inner worth.

If they could see what God sees, what a difference that would make! The Bible says ...

"From heaven the Lord looks down and sees all mankind; from his dwelling place he watches all who live on earth—he who forms the hearts of all, who considers everything they do." (Psalm 33:13–15)

Low self-worth can result from how you see/perceive yourself and how you think others see/perceive you. Faulty perceptions lead to faulty conclusions.

Faulty Perceptions and Faulty Conclusions

▶ Perfectionism: "I didn't do it right—I can't do anything right."

▶ Overgeneralization: "I failed, so I must be a failure."

▶ Overreacting: "I am horrible for having failed."

▶ False guilt: "I am the reason my dad left/died."

▶ Unforgiveness: "I can't forgive myself."

▶ Projection: "My mother didn't love me; therefore, no one will ever love me."

▶ Condemnation: "God could never forgive me."

▶ Unrealistic expectations: "I'll never measure up to what people expect of me."

▶ Fatalism: "No one believes I will ever amount to anything."

▶ Hopelessness: "There isn't anyone who holds out any hope for my life."

MYTH: "I will never be able to change the way I see myself and the way I think others see me."

TRUTH: Your faulty self-perception will automatically change as you fix your thoughts on the truth of Jesus.

> "Fix your thoughts on Jesus, the apostle and high priest whom we confess."
> (Hebrews 3:1)

Although Dorie never had a close friend at school, she tried. But even when she was out of the orphanage and in a foster home—she knew she looked different. One student pointed to her torn dress and jabbed, "Did that come out of the ark?" She forced a smile while the others laughed. Kids can be so cruel. Dorie confided, "How often I wished I could have spent the day in the restroom."[22] She just wanted to hide. The truth is: Dorie was just trying to survive the impact of a callous, cruel world without taking on the cynicism and bitterness of the world.

Whatever the contributing factors to your low estimation of your worth, they are held in place by wrong beliefs that you have embraced over the years. But the low opinion of yourself can be overcome by replacing those wrong beliefs with right beliefs.

> **"Do not conform any longer
> to the pattern of this world,
> but be transformed
> by the renewing of your mind.
> Then you will be able to test
> and approve what God's will is—
> his good, pleasing and perfect will."
> (Romans 12:2)**

WRONG BELIEF: "My self-worth is based on how I see myself in comparison to others and how others view me."

RIGHT BELIEF: "My self-worth is not based on how I see myself or how others see me, but on how God sees me, for I was created by Him in His image. Not only did Jesus pay the highest price for me by dying on the cross for my sins, but He also lives in me to fulfill His plan and purpose for me."

"We are God's workmanship, created in Christ Jesus to do good works, which God prepared in advance for us to do."
(Ephesians 2:10)

Dorie Van Stone says, "Let me encourage you to begin with God. Christ is the Wonderful Counselor, who can be trusted."[23] Money, education, possessions, and beauty are all things our society uses to gauge a person's worth. But we make a major mistake when we try to live by this value system. Why? Because it's hopelessly flawed. The world's value system is faulty because it's not the one God designed for us—the one He intended humans to live by when He created us *in His very own image.*

If you try to make it in the world's system, you may never measure up, and you will never have total security. However, you can find complete security by learning to adopt God's value system.

If you trust Him, God will begin to transform you from the inside out. Through His power, He will make you more like Him. He will make you the person you were always intended to be—*His precious child of infinite worth.* The Bible says ...

> "You received the Spirit of sonship.
> And by him we cry, '*Abba*, Father.'
> The Spirit himself testifies with our spirit
> that we are God's children.
> Now if we are children, then we are heirs—
> heirs of God and co-heirs with Christ."
> (Romans 8:15–17)

How to Have a Changed Life

Are you ready to believe what God says about you? Will you let Him change your view of yourself? Jesus said, *"You must be born again"* (John 3:7). But what does this mean? God has provided four truths that will help you understand your worth through a new birth.

Four Points of God's Plan:

#1 God's Purpose for You is *Salvation.*

What was God's motive in sending Christ to earth?

To express His love for you by saving you! The Bible says ...

"God so loved the world that he gave his one and only Son, that whoever believes in him shall not perish but have eternal life. For God did not send his Son into the world to condemn the world, but to save the world through him." (John 3:16–17)

What was Jesus' purpose in coming to earth?

To forgive your sins, empower you to have victory over sin, and enable you to live a fulfilled life! Jesus said ...

"I have come that they may have life, and have it to the full." (John 10:10)

#2 Your Problem is *Sin*.

What exactly is sin?

Sin is living independently of God's standard—knowing what is right, but choosing what is wrong. The Bible says ...

"Anyone, then, who knows the good he ought to do and doesn't do it, sins." (James 4:17)

What is the major consequence of sin?

Spiritual "death," eternal separation from God. Scripture states ...

"Your iniquities [sins] have separated you from your God. ... For the wages of sin is death, but the gift of God is eternal life in Christ Jesus our Lord." (Isaiah 59:2; Romans 6:23)

#3 God's Provision for You is the *Savior*.

Can anything remove the penalty for sin?

Yes! Jesus died on the cross to personally pay the penalty for your sins.

"God demonstrates his own love for us in this: While we were still sinners, Christ died for us." (Romans 5:8)

What can keep you from being separated from God?

Belief in (entrusting your life to) Jesus Christ as the only way to God the Father. Jesus says ...

"I am the way and the truth and the life. No one comes to the Father except through me." (John 14:6)

#4 Your Part is *Surrender.*

Give Christ control of your life—entrusting yourself to Him.

"Jesus said to his disciples, 'If anyone would come after me, he must deny himself and take up his cross [die to your own self-rule] and follow me. For whoever wants to save his life will lose it, but whoever loses his life for me will find it. What good will it be for a man if he gains the whole world, yet forfeits his soul?'" (Matthew 16:24–26)

Place your faith in (rely on) Jesus Christ as your personal Lord and Savior and reject your "good works" as a means of earning God's approval.

"It is by grace you have been saved, through faith—and this not from yourselves, it is the gift of God—not by works, so that no one can boast." (Ephesians 2:8–9)

The moment you choose to receive Jesus as your Lord and Savior—entrusting your life to Him—He comes to live inside you. Then He gives you His power to live the fulfilled life God has planned for you. If you want to be fully forgiven by God and become the person God created you to be, you can tell Him in a simple, heartfelt prayer like this:

PRAYER OF SALVATION

"God, I want a real relationship with You.
I admit that many times
I've chosen to go my own way
instead of Your way.
Please forgive me for my sins.
Jesus, thank You for dying on the cross
to pay the penalty for my sins.
Come into my life to be
my Lord and my Savior.
Change me from the inside out and make
me the person You created me to be.
In Your holy name I pray. Amen."

What Can You Expect Now?

If you sincerely prayed this prayer, you can know that you are forever a member of God's family, *forever loved* and *forever accepted* by Him!

"To all who received him [Jesus],
to those who believed in his name,
he gave the right to become children of God."
(John 1:12)

STEPS TO SOLUTION

One day at the orphanage, Dorie sat riveted at the back of a room hearing words she had never heard before—words foreign to her heart—words from a group of college students. But what Dorie heard couldn't be true! God didn't love her. God *couldn't* love her. *Nobody* loved her!

As the students prepared to leave, one of them turned around and spoke slowly with such sincerity that Dorie was stunned. The student said, "Even if you forget everything we have told you, remember—*God loves you*."

Though words can't explain it, she *knew* it was true, and she spoke directly to God. "They said you love me. Nobody else does. If you want me, you can have me!" That very instant an unexpected peace settled over her. She knew: *This must be God.*

At that point, she grabbed hold of that love and held on to God—and He never let her go. But even more, He says His love is never ending—for us all.[24] He says ...

"I have loved you with an everlasting love;
I have drawn you with loving-kindness."
(Jeremiah 31:3)

Key Passage to Read and Reread

Psalm 139

HOW TO KNOW YOUR REAL WORTH

▶ Realize that God knows all about you!
(vv. 1–6)

▶ Remember that God is always with you!
(vv. 7–12)

▶ Respect the fact that God created you!
(vv. 13–14)

▶ Recognize that God uniquely designed you!
(vv. 15–16)

▶ Receive God's loving thoughts toward you!
(vv. 17–18)

▶ Renounce God's enemies as enemies to you!
(vv. 19–22)

▶ Respond to God's changing you!
(vv. 23–24)

If you feel as though you have little value, is it possible your feelings are false? Remember the Bible says you are *"worth [your] weight in gold"* (Lamentations 4:2). Just think about how much *worth* that would literally be! If gold were selling at $250 per ounce, 1 pound (16 ounces) of gold would be worth $4,000. A person weighing 150 pounds would be worth $600,000—well over half a million dollars.[25]

Interestingly, the Bible presents a person's worth as too great to be measured in mere monetary terms. Peter says your faith alone is *"of greater worth than gold"* (1 Peter 1:7). Are you beginning to see how much *you*, combined with *your faith*, are worth in the eyes of God? You are indeed precious to God. You have God-given worth.

"How great is the love the Father has lavished on us, that we should be called children of God! And that is what we are!"
(1 John 3:1)

Pray, "Heavenly Father,
I confess my sin of (_____) to You,
and I am willing to turn from it.
Thank You for Your forgiveness.
I will rely on the power of Christ within me
to overcome my times of temptation.
Thank You for Your
grace and mercy toward me.
In Jesus name I pray. Amen."

Dorie understands the waves of guilt with which countless victims struggle. Victims of childhood sexual abuse typically struggle with guilt even though they are not guilty of the abuse. A reason for the ongoing after-the-fact guilt is that they think or wonder whether they could have taken actions to lessen or stop the abuse. And because everyone has periodic sin (not doing what is right in God's sight, whether in attitude or action), false guilt can get tangled together with true guilt.

Being pounded by *prolonged guilt* can strike a most damaging blow to your sense of worth, leaving you feeling dejected, discouraged, and demoralized. The problem with guilt is that it wears two faces—one is true, the other false.

▶ **False guilt** is Satan's way to shame you, condemn you, and produce disabling discouragement in you.

▶ **True guilt** is God's loving way to convict you, correct you, and conform you into the image of Christ so that you will reflect His character more accurately.

Godly sorrow over true guilt moves you to repentance, forgiveness, and freedom. Worldly sorrow produced by false guilt moves you to depression, despair, and death. In order to know how to get rid of your guilt, you need to identify whether it is true or false. Then you can respond accordingly.

**"Godly sorrow brings repentance that leads
to salvation and leaves no regret,
but worldly sorrow brings death."
(2 Corinthians 7:10)**

▶ **False guilt** arises when you blame yourself,
even though you've committed no wrong, or
when you continue to blame yourself after
you've confessed the wrong and turned from
your sin.

▶ **False guilt** is not resolved by confession because
it is not based on sin but on false accusations
aimed at making you feel unforgiven and
unaccepted by God. The truth is ...

**"The accuser of our brothers,
who accuses them before our God day and
night, has been hurled down."
(Revelation 12:10)**

▶ **False guilt** can be resolved by conferring with
wise, objective persons—mature Christians—
to help you determine whether the guilt you
are feeling is false. If it is false guilt, remind
yourself and your adversary Satan: (1) that
you are not guilty or (2) that you were guilty
but have been forgiven by God. The Bible
gives this assurance ...

**"There is now no condemnation
for those who are in Christ Jesus."
(Romans 8:1)**

▶ **True guilt** refers to the fact of your being at
fault.

▶ **True guilt** requires payment of a penalty so that fellowship with God and/or others can be restored.

▶ **True guilt** can be forgiven by God as you admit you have sinned and confess your sin to Him.

When you deal with your guilt God's way, God's Word says ...

> "As far as the east is from the west,
> so far has he removed
> our transgressions from us."
> (Psalm 103:12)

By the world's standards, Dorie had every right to hate her mother and harbor feelings of bitter unforgiveness. When her mother was charged with child neglect, Dorie had to appear in court. The judge asked her mother if Dorie was her child. After an agonizingly long pause, she answered, "Yes, but I'd have gotten rid of her before she was born if I could have!"[26]

The judge ordered Dorie and her sister permanently taken from their mother, and as they left the courtroom, her mother muttered to Dorie, "If I ever see you again, I'll kill you!" Dorie later said that her mother's rejection was total and final and all hope was quenched. "Am I that awful?" she asked herself. As she walked home alone, she prayed aloud that God would help her to understand why her mother had abandoned her, and she prayed that she wouldn't hate her mother.

Dorie said, "In that moment God let me forgive her. I felt sorry for her. I had no hatred. That day God performed a healing work in my life and prevented a permanent scar."[27] She was able to ...

"Get rid of all bitterness, rage and anger, brawling and slander, along with every form of malice." (Ephesians 4:31)

Do you struggle with low self-worth today because of poor parenting from your past? Are you floundering now because you had faulty authority figures? If so, leave behind those feelings of worthlessness, and experience your worth—the worth you have in the eyes of your heavenly Father. He wants you to:

▶ Admit the past truth.

▶ Address the present truth.

▶ Appropriate God's truth.

"Show me your ways, O Lord,
teach me your paths; guide me in your truth
and teach me, for you are God my Savior,
and my hope is in you all day long."
(Psalm 25:4–5)

Don't Let the Past Determine Your Present Worth

Using the list below, identify the parenting style by which you were raised. Then take the three appropriate steps to leave your feelings of worthlessness behind.

▶ **Overly critical parents/authority figures**

- *Admit the past truth*: "My parents were impossible to please."

- *Address the present truth*: "My worth is not based on pleasing people."

- *Appropriate God's truth*: "I am fully accepted by God."

"He made us accepted in the Beloved."
(Ephesians 1:6 NKJV)

▶ Overly protective parents/authority figures

- *Admit the past truth*: "I was smothered by my parents."

- *Address the present truth*: "My worth is not based on my ability to protect myself."

- *Appropriate God's truth*: "The Lord is my help in times of trouble."

"God is our refuge and strength, an ever-present help in trouble." (Psalm 46:1)

▶ Overly controlling parents/authority figures

- *Admit the past truth*: "I was not allowed to make my own decisions."

- *Address the present truth*: "My worth is not based on my decision making."

- *Appropriate God's truth*: "The Lord is my guide."

"God is our God for ever and ever; he will be our guide even to the end." (Psalm 48:14)

▶ Overly permissive parents/authority figures

- *Admit the past truth*: "My parents did not set firm boundaries for me."

- *Address the present truth*: "My worth is not based on my ability to set boundaries in my life."

- *Appropriate God's truth*: "The Lord has established my boundaries."

"You hem me in—behind and before; you have laid your hand upon me." (Psalm 139:5)

Forgive? Did God really expect Dorie to forgive all who mercilessly used and abused her, who treated her worse than a rabid animal, who withheld from her all the longings of her heart? Such a thing would be humanly impossible. Why would she even *want* to forgive the evil done to her? How *could* she ever forgive it? And why *should* she forgive it?

People with low self-worth often struggle to get past the circumstance that was the breeding ground for their low self-esteem. However, Dorie knew that in order to put the pieces of her broken life back together, it was necessary for her to forgive those who had grievously wronged her. The Bible says ...

> **"Bear with each other and forgive whatever grievances you may have against one another.**
> **Forgive as the Lord forgave you."**
> **(Colossians 3:13)**

Because the issue of forgiveness is such a stumbling block to so many people, let's understand that:

▶ **Forgiveness is not ...**

- Circumventing God's justice. God will execute His justice in His time and in His way.

- Letting the guilty off the hook. It is moving them from your hook onto God's hook.

- Excusing sinful behavior. God says the offense is without excuse.

- Stuffing your anger. It is resolving your anger by releasing it to God.

- Being a doormat. It is being like Christ—He is certainly not a doormat!

- Forgetting. It is essential to remember in order to forgive.

- A feeling. It is an act of the will.

"You need to persevere so that
when you have done the will of God,
you will receive what he has promised."
(Hebrews 10:36)

▶ **Forgiveness is ...**

- Dismissing a debt owed to you. It is releasing the offender from the obligation to repay you.

- Giving up the option of holding on to the offense. It is giving the offense to God.

- Possible without reconciliation. It is one-way and requires the action of only one person.

- Extended even if it is never requested or earned. It is in no way dependent on any action by the offender.

- Extending mercy. It is not giving the offender what is deserved.

- To set the offender free from you. It is to also set you free from the offender and free from bondage to bitterness.

- Changing your thinking about the offender. It is seeing the offender as someone in need of forgiveness, just as you are in need of forgiveness.

"The Lord our God is merciful and forgiving, even though we have rebelled against him." (Daniel 9:9)

▶ **Make a list of all persons you need to forgive.**

- Write down all offenses committed by each person.
- In prayer, one by one, release each offense to God.
- Take each offense off of your emotional hook and put them all onto God's hook.
- Then take the offender off of your hook and put that person onto God's hook.

"Never take revenge.
Leave that to the righteous anger of God.
For the Scriptures say, 'I will take revenge;
I will pay them back,' says the Lord."
(Romans 12:19 NLT)

FORGIVENESS PRAYER

"Lord Jesus, thank You for caring about
how much I have been hurt.
You know the pain I have felt
because of (<u>list each offense</u>).
Right now I release all that
pain into Your hands.
Thank You, Lord, for dying on the cross for
me and extending Your forgiveness to me.
As an act of my will,
I choose to forgive (<u>name</u>).
Right now, I take (<u>name</u>)
off of my emotional hook,
and I place (<u>name</u>) onto Your hook.
I refuse all thoughts of revenge.
I trust that in Your time and in Your way
You will deal with (<u>name</u>) as You see fit.
And Lord, thank You for giving me Your
power to forgive so that I can be set free.
In Your precious name I pray. Amen."

QUESTION: "How do I sustain a forgiving spirit?"

ANSWER: Most often, forgiveness is not a onetime event. You may need to go through many rounds of forgiving in your fight against bitterness. This is a normal part of the process of forgiveness. But if you confront your hurts and face your wounds, it will be worth the emotional bruises you will likely experience. As you consistently release each recurring thought of an offense or revenge for an offense, eventually the thoughts will diminish and disappear.

Dorie was constantly asked one question: "Aren't you bitter toward your mother?" And Dorie's consistent reply? "No. I am not. As a child in the orphanage, and the difficult years that followed, I experienced periods of bitterness, but I chose to forgive my mother even though I knew she would never respond to me. Perhaps the most basic mistake made by those who are bitter is the belief that they cannot forgive because they don't feel like it. Forgiveness is not an emotion. One can choose to forgive whether one feels like it or not. Many of us have had to reject our emotions, saying 'No' to our natural inclinations and firmly declare, 'I forgive.'"

Jesus emphasizes the "again and again" nature of forgiveness when He says …

> **"If he sins against you seven times in a day … forgive him."**
> **(Luke 17:4)**

For years Dorie concealed a secret. She thought people would not believe her if she told the sordid truth. After Dorie left the orphanage at age 13, she went into the first of many foster homes in which she suffered merciless verbal and emotional abuse, as well as physical and sexual abuse. She confided, "There was nothing I could do to stop him from violating my body. He warned me that if I ever told anyone he would kill me." Dorie believed him.[28]

At a later home, her rollaway bed was placed in a hallway where strange men passed by in the night. Her foster mother gave these men permission to perform immoral acts on Dorie, and she was repeatedly forced to participate in their perversions. As a result, she believed she could never be clean and whole again.

Dorie later said, "[God] gave the grace to bear my trials. It was He who chose me to belong to Him; He knew the first day of my life, as well as all the days in between. He knew that some day that dirty little girl would stand before thousands of people and tell them that God is faithful."[29]

Although Dorie van Stone experienced the depths of degradation and disgrace at the hands of those with the hardest of hearts, the Lord raised His choice servant up to bring hope to multitudes of people in America, on the mission field, and around the globe.

The Bible says …

> **"Though you have made me see troubles, many and bitter, you will restore my life again; from the depths of the earth you will again bring me up."**
> **(Psalm 71:20)**

It is possible for you to acquire a positive self-image and to learn to value yourself as God values you. In order to do that, God wants you to accept the following seven truths about yourself.

1 I accept God's Word that I was created in His image.

"God created man in his own image, in the image of God he created him; male and female he created them." (Genesis 1:27)

2 I accept myself as acceptable to Christ.

"Accept one another, then, just as Christ accepted you, in order to bring praise to God." (Romans 15:7)

3 I accept what I cannot change about myself.

"Who are you, O man, to talk back to God? 'Shall what is formed say to him who formed it, "Why did you make me like this?"' Does not the potter have the right to make out of the same lump of clay some pottery for noble purposes and some for common use?" (Romans 9:20–21)

4 I accept the fact that I will make mistakes.

"Not that I have already obtained all this, or have already been made perfect, but I press on to take hold of that for which Christ Jesus took hold of me. Brothers, I do not consider myself yet to have taken hold of it. But one thing I do: Forgetting what is behind and straining toward what is ahead, I press on toward the goal to win the prize for which God has called me heavenward in Christ Jesus." (Philippians 3:12–14)

5 I accept criticism and the responsibility for failure.

"I acknowledged my sin to you and did not cover up my iniquity. I said, 'I will confess my transgressions to the LORD'—and you forgave the guilt of my sin." (Psalm 32:5)

6 I accept the fact that I will not be liked or loved by everyone.

"If the world hates you, keep in mind that it hated me first. ... If they persecuted me, they will persecute you also." (John 15:18, 20)

7 I accept the unchangeable circumstances in my life.

"I have learned to be content whatever the circumstances." (Philippians 4:11)

Dorie's image of herself was shaped in part by her father, whom she met only after she became a young adult. Her time with him was limited, yet he was still a major influence on her sense of self-worth.

In Dorie's mind, she finally had the father she had longed for, and when she met with him to share her conviction that the Lord had called her to go as a missionary to New Guinea, she longed for his support and affirmation. Her sense of loss was profound when he answered, "If that's what you plan to do, then don't unpack your suitcase. From this moment on, you are not my daughter! I never want to see you again!"

As she traveled back home, she cried out to the Lord, "He was the only person in the world who ever loved me. How could he do this to me?" Her father had not only rejected her one last, painful time, but he had rejected Christ during that visit as well. Soon, however, Dorie had the presence of mind to remember that God had not left her. She was not alone. She said, "When you have nothing left but God, you realize that God is enough. God has stood beside me when no one else wanted me; He was not going to abandon me now. God would have to heal the emotional pain that throbbed through my body."

At that moment, Dorie began to allow the Lord to change her image of herself that had been perpetuated by her parents. She could choose to believe what the *Lord* said about her, not what her parents had said.[30] The Bible says ...

> "The Lᴏʀᴅ your God has chosen you out of all the peoples on the face of the earth to be his people, his treasured possession."
> (Deuteronomy 7:6)

1 If you say: "I just can't do anything right."

The Lord says: "I'll give you My strength to do what is right."

"I can do everything through him who gives me strength." (Philippians 4:13)

2 If you say: "I feel that I'm too weak."

The Lord says: "My power is perfect when you are weak."

"My grace is sufficient for you, for my power is made perfect in weakness." (2 Corinthians 12:9)

3 If you say: "I feel I'm not able to measure up."

The Lord says: "Rely on Me. I am able."

"God is able to make all grace abound to you, so that in all things at all times, having all that you need, you will abound in every good work." (2 Corinthians 9:8)

4 If you say: **"I don't feel that anyone loves me."**

The Lord says: "I love you."

"I have loved you with an everlasting love; I have drawn you with loving-kindness." (Jeremiah 31:3)

5 If you say: **"I can't forgive myself."**

The Lord says: "I can forgive you."

"I, even I, am he who blots out your transgressions, for my own sake, and remembers your sins no more." (Isaiah 43:25)

6 If you say: **"I wish I'd never been born."**

The Lord says: "Since before you were born, I've had plans for you."

"Before I formed you in the womb I knew you, before you were born I set you apart." (Jeremiah 1:5)

7 If you say: **"I feel my future is hopeless."**

The Lord says: "I know the future I have for you."

"'I know the plans I have for you,' declares the LORD, 'plans to prosper you and not to harm you, plans to give you hope and a future.'" (Jeremiah 29:11)

At times, do you feel inadequate, fearful, insecure—even when others say you shouldn't feel that way? If so, you're certainly not alone. When God first spoke to him, Moses was a man filled with insecurity and fear. In the burning bush the Lord supernaturally appeared to Moses instructing him to confront Pharaoh.

However, Moses argued with God. He felt he was a nobody with no authority, no credentials, no skills, and no confidence. Bottom line, he felt totally inadequate for the job and terrified of failing. And on top of all that, because he felt he couldn't speak well enough, he told God to send someone else! But God wouldn't accept his excuses. He told Moses ...

> "Who gave man his mouth?
> Who makes him deaf or mute?
> Who gives him sight or makes him blind?
> Is it not I, the LORD?
> Now go; I will help you speak
> and will teach you what to say."
> (Exodus 4:11–12)

Take comfort in this: God knows your limitations better than you do, and those limitations cannot impede the work the Lord has laid out for you. Just as God used Moses to lead an entire nation to freedom, God will work in and through you to accomplish His purposes for you. The Bible says you can be confident that ...

> "He who began a good work in you
> will carry it on to completion
> until the day of Christ Jesus."
> (Philippians 1:6)

When Dorie went to school, since she didn't have any lunch or money to buy lunch, during lunchtime she would say, "I'm going for a walk." Dorie confessed that if she had stayed in the lunchroom, "The sight of food would have been too much." The only clothes she owned were three tattered dresses and her scuffed shoes. To her, the thought that she was valuable was beyond comprehension. But oh, how wrong she was!

If you struggle with low self-worth, fully realize how *worthy* you are, and embrace these words as your personal goals:

> **"As a prisoner for the Lord, then,**
> **I urge you to live a life worthy**
> **of the calling you have received."**
> **(Ephesians 4:1)**

You Are WORInequality

You Are WORTHY

W ork on eliminating negative attitudes and beliefs.

"I will not hide my feelings or refuse to face them."

"I will not wallow in feelings of self-pity."

"I will not project my feelings onto others and become critical."

"Whatever is true, whatever is noble, whatever is right, whatever is pure, whatever is lovely, whatever is admirable—if anything is excellent or praiseworthy—think about such things." (Philippians 4:8)

O btain a scriptural understanding of having love for yourself.

"I am not to love myself with conceited love (pride)."

"I am to love the truth that God loves me and has a purpose for me."

- *Agape love* for myself: seeking God's highest purpose for me
- *Agape love* for others: seeking the highest good of another

"The entire law is summed up in a single command: 'Love your neighbor as yourself.'" (Galatians 5:14)

R efuse to compare yourself with others.

"I will not measure myself by others."

"I will thank God for what He has given me and what He is making of me."

"We do not dare to classify or compare ourselves with some who commend themselves." (2 Corinthians 10:12)

T hank God for His unconditional love for you.

"I will choose an attitude of thanksgiving even if I do not feel thankful."

"I will spend personal time with God, thanking Him for His unfailing love."

"We meditate on your unfailing love." (Psalm 48:9)

H ope with full assurance in God's promise to mold you to be more like Christ.

"I know that personal growth is a process."

"I know that God is committed to my growth."

"Those God foreknew he also predestined to be conformed to the likeness of his Son." (Romans 8:29)

Y ield your talents and abilities to helping others.

"I will be generous with my God-given gifts."

"I will realize my God-given worth as I focus on others."

"Each one should use whatever gift he has received to serve others, faithfully administering God's grace in its various forms." (1 Peter 4:10)

Dorie's childhood rejection was a seemingly impossible obstacle to overcome, at least as most people would view her life. Even though she had overcome much of her childhood pain, when her father died, some of the painful feelings of rejection and worthlessness resurfaced.

Upon hearing of her father's death, Dorie and her husband drove to Tulsa for his funeral. She signed the registry as his daughter and was stunned when the funeral director informed her that he had no children! The director insisted that her presence would upset the family, and she was turned away from the funeral home. Later, her aunt called and said the obituary had read "no children" and there would be discomfort for other family members if she appeared. Her father, even in death, had stung Dorie with yet another rejection—but this one delivered an even greater blow. She said, "My father's death ended all earthly ties with my relatives."[32]

However, Dorie did not lose her new sense of worth because of her father's rejection. She knew the Lord would always love her. The Lord had compassion toward her. The Lord would always be faithful to her. This was His promise of hope.

"I remember my affliction
and my wandering,
the bitterness and the gall.
I well remember them,
and my soul is downcast within me.
Yet this I call to mind
and therefore I have hope.
Because of the Lord's great love
we are not consumed,
for his compassions never fail."
(Lamentations 3:19–22)

Line Up Your Self-Image with God's Image of You

Your self-image has been greatly shaped predominantly by the messages you received and internalized from others, from your experiences, and from your own self-talk. When you were a child, you did not have control of those in authority over you, but since you are an adult, that is no longer the case. You are now able to choose those with whom you associate, and you can certainly control your self-talk. Therefore, you can take an active part in changing the distorted view you have of yourself.

▶ **Accept yourself.**

- Stop striving for perfection or trying to be like someone else.

- Realize the Lord made you for a purpose, and He designed your personality and gave you the gifts and abilities He wanted you to have in order to accomplish His purpose for you.

"The LORD will fulfill his purpose for me."
(Psalm 138:8)

▶ Thank God for encouraging you.

- Acknowledge and praise God for the abilities He has given you and the things He has accomplished through you.

- Engage in biblically-based, encouraging self-talk and mute the condemning critic inside your head.

"May our Lord Jesus Christ himself and God our Father, who loved us and by his grace gave us eternal encouragement and good hope, encourage your hearts and strengthen you in every good deed and word."
(2 Thessalonians 2:16–17)

▶ Accept the compliments of others.

- To discount the positive comments of those who have heartfelt appreciation for you is to discount their opinions and their desire to express their gratitude to you.

- Practice graciously accepting compliments and turning them into praise to God for the affirmation that He is at work in you and producing good "fruit" through you.

"This is to my Father's glory, that you bear much fruit, showing yourselves to be my disciples."
(John 15:8)

▶ **Release the negative past and focus on a positive future.**

- Refuse to dwell on negative things said or done to you in the past and release them to God.

- Embrace the work God is doing in your life now and cooperate with him by focusing on Him and on His character. Trust in His promise to fulfill His purposes in you.

"It is God who works in you to will and to act according to his good purpose." (Philippians 2:13)

▶ **Live in God's forgiveness.**

- God has extended forgiveness to you for all of your sins (past, present, and future). Confess and repent of anything offensive to God. Do not set yourself up as a higher judge than God by refusing to forgive yourself.

- Lay harsh judgment of yourself aside and accept that you will not be made "fully perfect" and totally without sin until you stand in the presence of Christ and are fully conformed to His image.

"We are children of God, and what we will be has not yet been made known. But we know that when he appears, we shall be like him, for we shall see him as he is. Everyone who has this hope in him purifies himself, just as he is pure." (1 John 3:2–3)

▶ **Benefit from your mistakes.**

- Realize that you can learn from your mistakes, as well as from the mistakes of others, and decide to view your mistakes as opportunities to learn needed lessons.

- Ask God what He wants to teach you from your mistakes, listen to Him, and learn from Him. Then move forward with a positive attitude and practice actions based on the insights you have gained.

"We know that in all things God works for the good of those who love him, who have been called according to his purpose." (Romans 8:28)

▶ **Form supportive, positive relationships.**

- Realize that critical people are hurt people who project their own feelings of inadequacy onto others in an attempt to ease their own emotional pain.

- Minimize the time you spend with negative, critical people, whether family, friends, or coworkers, and seek out those who encourage and support you both emotionally and spiritually.

"He who walks with the wise grows wise, but a companion of fools suffers harm." (Proverbs 13:20)

▶ **Formulate realistic goals and plans.**

- Elicit the help of others to identify your strengths/weaknesses and the gifts God has given you, as well as the things that you are persuaded God has called you to do.

- Prayerfully set some reasonable, achievable goals that capitalize on your strengths, and make a plan as to how you will set about to accomplish those goals.

"Do you not know that in a race all the runners run, but only one gets the prize? Run in such a way as to get the prize." (1 Corinthians 9:24)

▶ **Identify your heart's desires.**

- Make a list of the things you have dreamed of doing but have never attempted because of a fear of failure or a lack of self-assurance.

- Share each desire with the Lord, asking Him to confirm to you which ones are from Him. Then lay out the steps you need to take in order to move toward fulfilling them.

"Delight yourself in the LORD and he will give you the desires of your heart." (Psalm 37:4)

▶ **Plan for success.**

- Anticipate any obstacles to accomplishing your goals and desires and plan strategies for overcoming them.

- Think of yourself as achieving each goal and doing the things God has put on your heart to do.

"May he give you the desire of your heart and make all your plans succeed." (Psalm 20:4)

▶ **Celebrate each accomplishment.**

- Your feeling of self-worth and self-confidence will grow with the acknowledgement of each accomplishment.

- Rejoice with the Lord and other significant people over the things God and you have done together. Affirm and celebrate your success.

"There, in the presence of the LORD your God, you and your families shall eat and shall rejoice in everything you have put your hand to, because the LORD your God has blessed you." (Deuteronomy 12:7)

At some point Dorie wrote, "I heard the voice of God—the voice that had whispered to me during those many years of loneliness, sorrow, and heartache: 'Dorie, your end is going to be so much better than your beginning.'"[33] And how true! Not only did Christ accept Dorie just as she was, but He also elevated her to be His representative, His voice, His ambassador. To her amazement, Dorie now has experienced firsthand these precious words from the Psalms:

> **"He raises the poor from the dust**
> **and lifts the needy from the ash heap;**
> **he seats them with princes,**
> **with the princes of their people."**
> **(Psalm 113:7–8)**

Mistreatment is no stranger to any of us. Why then, in the face of misfortune, do some victims see themselves as having little value, while others live victoriously in light of their true value? What makes the difference? The victorious Christian learns priceless lessons through mistreatment.

▶ **Allow** your mistreatment to be the making of your ministry.

"The Father of compassion and the God of all comfort ... comforts us in all our troubles, so that we can comfort those in any trouble with the comfort we ourselves have received from God." (2 Corinthians 1:3–4)

▶ **Don't be consumed with the negatives** you have received from others.

"Forget the former things; do not dwell on the past. See, I am doing a new thing! Now it springs up; do you not perceive it? I am making a way in the desert and streams in the wasteland." (Isaiah 43:18–19)

▶ **Be consumed with the positives** you have received from God—positives He will lead you to pass on to others.

The blessing comes when you focus not on what you are getting, but on what you are giving. Jesus suffered immense mistreatment, yet He was not burdened with low self-worth. His ministry of compassion models for us the truth that truly, *"It is more blessed to give than to receive"* (Acts 20:35).

"God wanted to prove that He can take care of a dirty, unwanted child. He could help me endure the beatings, the sexual abuse, and the rejection from my father as well as from my mother. God wanted to prove a point, and He did. Now I have the privilege of telling thousands of people that God can take 'nobodys' and make them into 'somebodys' for His name's sake."[34]

—Dorie Van Stone

At an auction, how is the worth of an item determined? Only by the highest price paid. Jesus paid the highest price possible— He gave His life to give you life. This priceless sacrifice established your worth forever!

—June Hunt

SCRIPTURES TO MEMORIZE

How can you know whether **you are valuable** or **not**?

"Look at the birds of the air; they do not sow or reap or store away in barns, and yet your heavenly Father feeds them. Are you not much more valuable than they?" (Matthew 6:26)

How does God feel about us if **we** are **called children of God**?

"How great is the love the Father has lavished on us, that we should be called children of God!" (1 John 3:1)

Do we have to change before **God** will have **love for us**?

"God demonstrates his own love for us in this: While we were still sinners, Christ died for us." (Romans 5:8)

If you think God has never **loved you** or **drawn you**, do you know what He actually says about you?

"I have loved you with an everlasting love; I have drawn you with loving-kindness." (Jeremiah 31:3)

How do we overcome our feelings that **we are not competent**?

"Not that we are competent in ourselves to claim anything for ourselves, but our competence comes from God." (2 Corinthians 3:5)

When **we compare ourselves** with other people, **are** we **wise**—or **not**?

> *"**We** do not dare to classify or **compare ourselves** with some who commend themselves. When they measure themselves by themselves and compare themselves with themselves, they **are not wise**."* (2 Corinthians 10:12)

How could **He forgive us** for **our sins** and the stupid things we've done?

> *"If we confess our sins, **he** is faithful and just and will **forgive us our sins** and purify us from all unrighteousness."* (1 John 1:9)

Would God ever say to me, that my life was a "mistake"—even **before** I **came to be** born?

> *"Your eyes saw my unformed body. All the days ordained for me were written in your book **before** one of them **came to be**."* (Psalm 139:16)

How can we overcome thinking or feeling we weren't **created to do** anything **good**?

> *"We are God's workmanship, **created** in Christ Jesus **to do good** works, which God prepared in advance for us to do."* (Ephesians 2:10)

Should there ever be a sense of **condemnation for those who are in Christ**?

> *"There is now no **condemnation for those who are in Christ** Jesus."* (Romans 8:1)

NOTES

1. Doris Van Stone with Erwin Lutzer, *Dorie: The Girl Nobody Loved* (Chicago: Moody Press, 1979).

2. Van Stone and Lutzer, *Dorie*, 11–15.

3. *Merriam-Webster Online Dictionary,* s.v. "Worth"; http://www.m-w.com.

4. Naji Abi-Hashem, "Self-Esteem," in *Baker Encyclopedia of Psychology & Counseling*, 2nd ed., ed. David G. Benner and Peter C. Hill (Grand Rapids: Baker, 1999), 1085.

5. Johannes P. Louw, Eugene Albert Nida, *Greek-English Lexicon of the New Testament: Based on Semantic Domains*, electronic ed. of the 2nd edition (New York: United Bible societies, 1996) 1:621.

6. Van Stone and Lutzer, *Dorie*, 28–29.

7. *Merriam-Webster Online Dictionary*, s.v. "Esteem."

8. Robert Laird Harris, Gleason Leonard Archer, Bruce Waltke, *Theological Wordbook of the Old Testament*, electronic ed. (Chicago: Moody Press, 1999), s.v. "hasab"; James Swanson, *Dictionary of Biblical Languages With Semantic Domains: Hebrew (Old Testament)*, electronic ed. (Oak Harbor : Logos Research Systems, Inc., 1997), s.v. "hasab."

9. *Merriam-Webster Online Dictionary*, s.v. "Self-Esteem."

10. Van Stone and Lutzer, *Dorie*, 13.

11. *Merriam-Webster Online Dictionary*, s.v. "Complex, Inferior, Inferiority Complex."

12. Van Stone and Lutzer, *Dorie*, 19–20.

13. For quotations and allusions in this section see Van Stone and Lutzer, *Dorie*, 17–26.

14. Van Stone and Lutzer, *Dorie*, 23.

15. Van Stone and Lutzer, *Dorie*, 20.

16. Van Stone and Lutzer, *Dorie*, 21.

17. Van Stone and Lutzer, *Dorie*, 27.

18. Van Stone and Lutzer, *Dorie*, 29.

19. Van Stone and Lutzer, *Dorie*, 29.

20. Van Stone and Lutzer, *Dorie*, 27–30.

21. Van Stone and Lutzer, *Dorie*, 29.

22. Van Stone and Lutzer, *Dorie*, 44.

23. Doris Van Stone, *Dorie: The Girl Nobody Loved*, VHS (Chattanooga, TN: Precept Ministries, 1990).

24. For quotations and allusions in this section see Van Stone and Lutzer, *Dorie*, 30.

25. One pound equals .454 kilograms. One hundred and fifty pounds equals 68.1 kilograms.

26. Van Stone and Lutzer, *Dorie*, 48.

27. Van Stone and Lutzer, *Dorie*, 48.

28. Van Stone and Lutzer, *Dorie*, 147–148.

29. Doris Van Stone and Edwin W. Lutzer, *No Place to Cry: The Hurt and Healing of Sexual Abuse* (Chicago, Moody Press, 1990), 24, 26.

30. Van Stone and Lutzer, *Dorie*, 78.

31. *Creating Self-Esteem and Self-Confidence*, VHS (Huntsville, TX: Educational Video Network, 1999).

32. Van Stone and Lutzer, *Dorie*, 91–93.

33. Van Stone, *Dorie*, VHS.

34. Van Stone and Lutzer, *No Place to Cry*, 119.

SELECTED BIBLIOGRAPHY

Abi-Hashem, Naji. "Self-Esteem." In *Baker Encyclopedia of Psychology & Counseling*, 2nd ed, edited by David G. Benner and Peter C. Hill, 1084–1087. Grand Rapids: Baker, 1999.

Adams, Jay E. *The Biblical View of Self-Esteem, Self-Love, Self-Image*. Eugene, OR: Harvest House, 1986.

Allen, Ronald B. *The Majesty of Man*. Portland, OR: Multnomah, 1984.

Andersen, Hans Christian. *The Ugly Duckling*, 1844. http://hca.gilead.org.il/ugly_duc.html.

Brand, Paul, and Philip Yancey. *Fearfully and Wonderfully Made*. Grand Rapids: Zondervan, 1980.

Brand, Paul, and Philip Yancey. *In His Image*. Grand Rapids: Judith Markham, 1984.

Crabb, Lawrence J., Jr. *Understanding People: Deep Longings for Relationship*. Ministry Resources Library. Grand Rapids: Zondervan, 1987.

Hunt, June. *Counseling Through Your Bible Handbook*. Eugene, Oregon: Harvest House Publishers, 2008.

Hunt, June. *How to Forgive . . . When You Don't Feel Like It*. Eugene, Oregon: Harvest House Publishers, 2007.

Hunt, June. *How to Handle Your Emotions*. Eugene, Oregon: Harvest House Publishers, 2008.

Hunt, June. *Seeing Yourself Through God's Eyes.* Eugene, Oregon: Harvest House Publishers, 2008.

Manning, Brennan. *Abba's Child: The Cry of the Heart for Intimate Belonging.* Colorado Springs, CO: NavPress, 1994.

Mayo, Mary Ann. *Skin Deep: Understanding the Powerful Link between Your Body Image and Your Self-Esteem.* Ann Arbor, MI: Vine, 1992.

McGee, Robert S. *The Search for Significance.* 2nd ed. Houston, TX: Rapha, 1990.

McGinnis, Alan Loy. *Confidence: How to Succeed at Being Yourself.* Minneapolis, MN: Augsburg, 1987.

Stowell, Joseph M. *Perilous Pursuits.* Chicago: Moody, 1994.

Van Stone, Doris. *Dorie: The Girl Nobody Loved.* VHS. Chattanooga, TN: Precept Ministries, 1990.

Van Stone, Doris, and Erwin W. Lutzer. *No Place to Cry.* Chicago: Moody, 1990.

VanVonderen, Jeff. *Tired of Trying to Measure Up.* Minneapolis, MN: Bethany House, 1989.

HOPE FOR THE HEART TITLES

www.aspirepress.com

The HOPE FOR THE HEART Biblical Counseling Library is Your Solution!

- Easy-to-read, perfect for anyone.
- Short. Only 96 pages. Good for the busy person.
- Christ-centered biblical advice and practical help
- Tested and proven over 20 years of June Hunt's radio ministry
- 30 titles in the series – each tackling a key issue people face today.
- Affordable. You or your church can give away, lend, or sell them.

Display available for churches and ministries.

www.aspirepress.com